THE STORY OF TEXAS

9/03

THE STORY OF
TEXAS

Text by John Edward Weems
Compiled by Ron Stone

Illustrated by Tom Jones

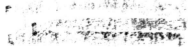

SHEARER PUBLISHING
FREDERICKSBURG • TEXAS

Amarillo

Lubbock

Midland
Odessa

pine

San Angelo

Del Rio

Laredo

Stephen F. Austin

Sam Houston

Dallas

Fort Worth

Tyler

Nacogdoches

Austin

Bryan/College Station

Beaumont

Houston

San Antonio

Victoria

Corpus Christi

Brownsville

Texarkana

Gulf of
Mexico

THE STATE OF TEXAS

6 - 1986

TO THE PARENT

"How can I make my child a reader?" One of the best ways is by providing fun, interesting books for his or her very own. Books in the home help develop good reading habits and skills which are fundamental to your child's success in school and throughout the years ahead. At bedtime, in a car or bus, taking the time to read to your child says a lot. It says, "I love books and reading and I want to share this love with you." Please remember that children who develop good reading habits acquire and use knowledge more efficiently and effectively!

CONTENTS

PART 1:
THE BEGINNING

I magine much of the vast and varied region now called Texas as covered by greenish waters of a sea that looked like the Gulf of Mexico. Countless ages ago much of what is now Texas did indeed lie at the bottom of a large body of water.

Now imagine that soaked area as emerging from the sea over a very long period of time, and later giving root space and growth to flowers, grasses, weeds. Fresh water falling from low clouds greened the sun-spattered plants. This, too, happened.

Imagine more. Think of Texas during that

dimly known, prehistoric time as inhabited only by animal life, not by any human beings. Men and women came later to North America and to Texas from some other part of the world. Possibly the first humans came to North America from Asia, across a natural bridge of land that once existed in the Bering Strait, between what are now Russia and Alaska. From there they came on to Texas and other places.

The first human beings to make that journey were hunters — adventurers who liked being on the move, not farmer-types who preferred to stay in one place and raise crops. But the farmers came later, and after the passage of many years, those earliest immigrants were represented in Texas by many different groups or tribes. Eventually they were called "Indians" when Christopher Columbus arrived in North America in 1492 and thought he had reached the Indies.

Indians differed greatly from nation to nation and from tribe to tribe in how they looked, what they wore, what they ate, and how they lived.

They were the first Texans, but they all came from some other land. Texans of later days also came from somewhere else, of course, so that people of many races, religions, and beliefs live together now as citizens of Texas.

Indians sometimes left drawings, called pictographs, on rocks and in caves to illustrate their mode of living and the exciting events in which they took part. But most of what is known about those now-vanished early immigrants has come from accounts and descriptions by scientists who have gathered evidence by digging into long-buried Indian sites.

Scientists have discovered recently that human life existed in Texas even earlier than they used to believe. Some of their guesses about the first human presence in Texas go back in time ten or twelve thousand years, and even before that.

Bones indicate that some of these people looked very different from today's Indians.

Much easier to determine is the date of arrival in Texas of the first Europeans, who were attracted by fascinating stories of the "New World" told by

Christopher Columbus and other explorers. Many of the Europeans wrote stories about the wondrous things they saw, so the recorded history of Texas began with the arrival of those adventurers.

In 1519 a Spaniard named Alonso Álvarez de Piñeda led a group of men who mapped the coastline of the Gulf of Mexico from Florida to Vera Cruz, but Piñeda and his explorers didn't venture any distance inland into Texas.

The first man who saw much of Texas and wrote about it was another Spaniard, Alvar Núñez Cabeza de Vaca. But his journey was the result of an unfortunate accident.

Cabeza de Vaca was a member of a Spanish expedition that sailed from Cuba to Florida in 1527 with the aim of conquering and colonizing part of the Gulf Coast. The commander, Pánfilo de Narváez, and Cabeza de Vaca and about 250 other expedition members left the ships to explore the land. They failed to arrive at a designated harbor in time to meet the ships that were supposed to pick them up. The vessels sailed without them.

The Spaniards left behind were isolated in a strange land, with little knowledge of it that would enable them to survive like the natives who called the place home. But Pánfilo de Narváez knew that other Spaniards had established a settlement named Pánuco on the Gulf Coast far to the west, near what is now Tampico, in Old Mexico — or

"New Spain," as it was known then. He intended to get his men there by following the Gulf coastline.

Narváez ordered his men to build five boats from whatever materials they could find. The craft proved to be crude, frail, and barely seaworthy. But the men collected some food, embarked, and set out westward, following one grim sunset after another along the low coastline.

Despair soon conquered most of them. They were existing on a daily ration of "half a handful of raw maize," Cabeza de Vaca wrote later. Stormy autumn weather chilled them, even in that moderate climate.

One particularly clouded sunset seemed likely to be the last one for the men in Cabeza de Vaca's boat. All but five of them were so weak from hunger and exposure to violent weather they appeared to be more dead than alive as the hours passed.

During a dreadfully dark night only Cabeza de Vaca was well enough to handle the boat.

The coming of another dawn announced itself with only a very dull light, but with a steady roaring noise that startled Cabeza de Vaca. It proved to be "the tumbling of the sea" — a heavy surf.

"Near the shore a wave took us, that knocked the boat out of water the distance of the throw of a crowbar, and from the violence with which she struck, nearly all the people who were in her like dead, were roused to consciousness. Finding themselves near the shore, they began to move on hands and feet, crawling to land. . . . There we

made fire, parched some of the maize we brought, and found some rain water."

Cabeza de Vaca wrote that the day of their storm-tossed arrival on this island was November 6, 1528. He and his companions named the place Malhado, which is a Spanish word meaning "misfortune." Many historians believe the place where they landed was today's Galveston Island.

The parched maize and fresh water revived the unlucky, starving Spaniards to some extent. One man climbed a tree and reported that the boat had indeed come ashore on an island. Then he looked around further, found empty Indian huts, and from them took a clay cooking pot, a small dog, and some fish.

Three Indians carrying bows and arrows appeared a short distance away and followed the man as he returned to his companions. Then the natives stopped, sat on the sandy beach, and stared at the Spaniards. Half an hour later the three warriors were joined by a hundred others.

The Spaniards stared back and realized they were helpless — "for it would have been difficult," Cabeza de Vaca wrote, "to find six [of our men] that could rise from the ground." The longer the Spaniards stared, the larger those Indians appeared to be, until, finally, they seemed to be giants.

Cabeza de Vaca and another Spaniard gathered up some trinkets, walked a short distance toward the Indians, and called to them. The warriors approached, and the two Spaniards handed out the showy little things — hawkbells and beads. Each Indian then gave Cabeza de Vaca an arrow, standing for friendship. The Indians also indicated they would return soon with food, and they did.

But most of the Spaniards were already so ill that they soon died. Eventually Cabeza de Vaca spent six years of captivity among the natives before gaining freedom. He spent another two years wandering across Texas and other strange lands before arriving, with three other survivors, at the Spanish outpost of Culiacán, near the Gulf of California, on May 18, 1536.

Later, his writing brought other explorers to the strange wilderness, in search of supposed riches to be found there. One was Francisco Vásquez de Coronado, who led a large expedition of fourteen hundred Spaniards and Indians toward a talked-of Seven Cities of Cíbola. But these "golden cities" existed only in the gossip and imagination of men dreaming of great wealth available for the taking.

Coronado also searched for a golden land called Quivira that an Indian slave told him lay far to the eastward. Coronado marched for two and a half months looking for it, traveling across part of the flat and treeless plains of what is now the Texas Panhandle during his search. Finally he found Quivira, which consisted of several Wichita Indian grass-shack villages situated in what is now central Kansas. Not even the chief wore any gold. He wore only a copper plate about his neck.

Coronado's report discouraged any more Spanish exploration in the region. Spaniards never did occupy and colonize what is now the state of Texas to any great extent. But Spanish influence was, and still is, felt. The flag of Spain was the first of six national ensigns to fly over Texas.

The second flag came from France, but French explorers left few marks on the state. In 1685 René Robert Cavelier, Sieur de La Salle sought to establish a French colony on Matagorda

Bay, in Texas. He also intended to explore the area with the aim of taking it permanently for King Louis XIV of France.

Mistakes and misfortunes doomed his attempt. La Salle was able to establish a fort named St. Louis, possibly on Garcitas Creek near Matagorda Bay. He meant to leave a permanent French Colony there. But in 1687 he was killed by some of his own discontented men during an exploring journey. Two years later Indians attacked Fort St. Louis and left it in ruins.

La Salle was important in Texas history for making the Spaniards suspicious of the French and for convincing them they should make a greater effort to occupy Texas in order to hold it. For this reason Spaniards established posts and missions in a previously unoccupied land that is now East Texas. It was known then as the land of the friendly "Tejas" Indians, from whom Texas got its name.

Actually, there was no tribe of Indians named Tejas. The natives referred to were Hasinai, a group of Caddoan Indians. But they greeted the first European explorers with the word, "Tejas," meant to indicate friendship.

Only a short distance farther east and north of East Texas lay a large territory claimed by France in those days. For a while the suspicious Spaniards watched out for French traders coming into the Spanish realm with the supposed intention of taking away riches belonging to the king of Spain. But the main threat to Spain came eventually from the United States.

In 1762 France gave its large territory, Louisiana, to Spain, to avoid having to sign ownership away to a hated enemy, Great Britain. France had just lost a war to the British.

The adventurers who then began trespassing on this vast Spanish domain west of the Mississippi River were mostly Anglo-Americans. In 1801 the first explorer from the United States to travel great distances into Spanish lands and to map them was killed by Spanish troops near what is now Blum, in Hill County, Texas. He was Philip Nolan, a native of Ireland who had physical strength, courage, and charm that officials in New Spain had come to fear. To prove Nolan was dead, his slayers cut off his ears and sent them to the Spanish governor at San Antonio. Nolan's twenty-four men were captured.

One of those captives spent the next ten years in a series of dismal prisons deep in Mexico. For a long time his only companion and friend was a white lizard that he found, tamed, and trained.

The name of this captured American was Peter Ellis Bean, a native of Tennessee. Bean was only seventeen years old when the Spaniards took him after Philip Nolan's death. But Bean had intelligence, experience, and charm unusual for a person that young. He had little formal schooling,

however, and he never learned to write well. Later someone helped him write the story of his life, and in it he told about his jail friend, the white lizard.

He found it in a Mexican city, Acapulco, that most American visitors to the place think of today as offering fun and excitement. It is a famed tourist resort. But when Bean and other prisoners were marched across Mexico to Acapulco in the early 1800's, they saw very little of the beauty of the place.

MARTIAL DRESS DURING THE SPANISH ASCENDANCY IN THE NEW WORLD.

Spanish guards took Bean and other prisoners, all in irons, through the town and up a hill to a huge old castle named San Diego that overlooked the bay. From atop San Diego's towering stone walls a hundred guns pointed toward the blue Pacific Ocean and the bay. The Spaniards were ready to repel any foe that threatened Acapulco.

Inside the castle itself Spaniards had cells for holding any foe caught threatening their empire in the New World. They considered young Bean as such a threat, so they took him to that prison. Bean and others stood waiting at the moat that encircled the castle.

Soon some men inside noisily lowered a great drawbridge, and the prisoners and their guards

2.

walked across it. Then there followed a series of
metallic creaks and groans, and the drawbridge
came up again. For young Bean it was a long way
back to his home in Tennessee.

Bean's captors locked him in a dark, narrow,
stone cell about three feet wide and seven feet
long. They left his irons on him. At the far end of
the cell, light shone dimly through a small, grated
opening built high up in the twelve-foot wall. A little more light entered through another small opening in the cell door.

For three months Bean stayed alone in the
cell. Every day a guard brought him "a pot of
water, and some beef and bread." But Bean never
stopped hoping for escape. Then, at the end of

three months, Bean's jail companion appeared.
Years later Bean remembered and wrote about it.

"... There is here a lizard ... about nine or
ten inches long and about three inches thick. It is

as white as snow, and, if you hold it between you and the light, you may see the bones in its limbs and body. One day, as I was lying on my mat, I saw one of them, for the first time, on the wall. Watching him, I saw that he was trying to catch the flies that had come into the prison when the door was opened, to get out of the sun. I did not know whether he was poisonous or not, but I determined to feed him. So I caught some flies, and put them on the end of a straw I had pulled out of my mat; these I slipped up the wall to him, and found he would take them off the straw. This was my amusement for some days, when he became so gentle that he would take flies off my hand. Every morning, as he came down the wall, he would sing like a frog, by which means I [noticed] that he was coming. In about a week he was so gentle, that he did not leave me at night, but stayed with me all the time. Every day, when they would open the door to come and examine my irons, he would get frightened, and hide himself under my blanket. When the door was again shut, he would come out and stay with me. I found that he was sincerely my friend; in fact, he was my only companion and amusement."

Once, Bean was taken from his cell to a hospital. After an absence of several days he returned.

"The next day my lizard came down the wall, and as soon as I saw him I reached out my hand for him to come on it, but he was afraid . . . . It was four or five days before I could get him to know me; then he was as friendly as ever . . ."

One day Bean managed to escape while he

was working, under guard, outside the castle. But he was recaptured in a few days.

Back in his cell again, he looked for his lizard without success. Finally, two days later, Bean wrote, the lizard "came down the wall; but he had got wild, and would not come to me. At last I caught him, and he became as gentle as usual."

Bean left his pet lizard for good when Mexico rebelled against Spain in 1810. His Spanish captors released him and other prisoners on their promise to fight the rebels. But Bean immediately deserted to the Mexicans. That revolution failed, but Bean continued to work for the defeated rebels. In 1821 Mexico finally won independence from Spain, partly with Bean's help.

I n Texas, many things had changed while Bean had been in prison. France had forced Spain to give back the land around Texas called Louisiana. Then France had sold that land in 1803 to the United States, in what became known as the "Louisiana Purchase." But Texas continued under Spanish domination until 1821 — the year Mexico won independence. After that the Mexican flag flew over Texas for fifteen years, until 1836. It was the third of those six flags that have flown over the Lone Star State.

But the Mexican government found an early problem in Texas. Hostile Indians roamed free over much of that land and prevented its settlement. Mexico wanted prosperity in

Texas, for the sake of the entire nation. Despite this, Mexico couldn't persuade many of its own citizens to move to Texas to reach this goal.

For that reason the Mexican government accepted a plan from a bright, educated, diplomatic

young native of the United States. His name was Stephen F. Austin.

Austin received permission to bring three hundred families from the United States to a large, fertile block of land lying along the Texas Gulf Coast and farther inland from there. Later, other Anglo-Americans received similar permission.

In return, Austin and the other colonists promised to adhere to the Catholic faith and to other Mexican ideals. Austin sincerely tried to do this and worked to see that the other colonists did, too.

Immigrants came in ever-growing numbers. They arrived in vessels that sailed from New Orleans across the Gulf of Mexico to some landfall on the Texas coast. They came by land, entering

Texas through the old Spanish town of Nacogdoches, built deep in the pine woods. They also came by land lying farther to the north, along the Red River.

Most of the earliest Anglo-Americans lived in hurriedly built log cabins with floors of dirt or clay, or sometimes split logs with the flat sides facing upward. The clothes they wore were either homespun or brought from the United States. The food most of them ate was provided by their own hands. They killed and butchered wild game or cattle or hogs, baked a coarse bread from cornmeal, and grew sweet potatoes for their meals. But they ate few other vegetables.

They drank strong coffee, usually black. Sometimes shortages forced them to brew it from some poor substitute, like ground corn. Oddly, they rarely drank fresh milk, even when they owned cows. Butter was also scarce. Occasionally they drank, or served, buttermilk in place of coffee.

During the hot and humid summers it was impossible for them to keep food cold. The invention of refrigeration lay many years in the future.

There were no schools. The few early immigrants who had money enough to educate their children sent them to the United States or arranged for their education at home.

So many immigrants came to Texas from the United States that Mexican officials began to worry about their ability to hold on to the land. They began imposing restrictions and taxes on the colonists. At first Stephen F. Austin supported Mexico, but even he became angry.

Rebellion broke out in Texas. The colonists chose a recent immigrant, Sam Houston, to lead them. Houston, a tall and impressive man, had been a leader in his native Tennessee.

Other men whose names became famous came to Texas to fight in the rebellion: William Barret Travis, Jim Bowie, Davy Crockett, James Fannin, James Bonham.

But not all the rebels were Anglo-American. Some persons with Mexican names also fought for Texas independence. They, too, had been angered by government restrictions, and many of them didn't like the man who had become dictator of Mexico and of all its outlying territory, including Texas.

The dictator's name was Antonio López de Santa Anna. Santa Anna was an able general, trained by Spanish officers before Mexican inde-

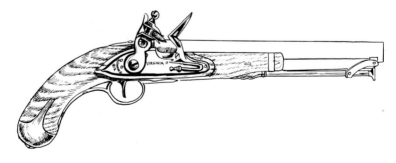

pendence. But he could be slippery, moody, and cruel. Before coming to Texas, Santa Anna had crushed rebellions inside Mexico with a savagery that turned many of his own countrymen against him.

On February 23, 1836, Santa Anna and the first units of a Mexican army that eventually totaled five thousand soldiers arrived in San Antonio. They intended to stamp out the Texas rebellion without wasting much time.

First, they planned to destroy a Texas force of fewer than two hundred men who had locked themselves inside an old, abandoned Spanish mission called the Alamo, in San Antonio. A high wall surrounded it, and at least eighteen artillery pieces defended it.

Inside, the commander, William Barret Travis, hurriedly wrote a message pleading for help from other Texas rebels. Then he put it in the hands of a messenger who mounted a horse and rode out of the Alamo heading eastward, toward the rebellious settlements.

A short distance away the messenger paused

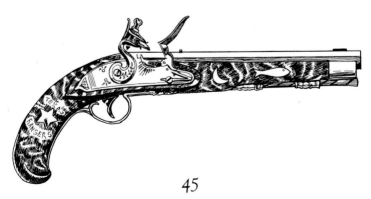

for a last look backward at San Antonio. He saw a fearful sight. Units of General Santa Anna's cavalry were filling the city's Military Plaza. Their breastplates reflected the dazzling afternoon sun.

During the next two weeks only thirty-two men, volunteers from the town of Gonzales nearby, sneaked past the Mexican army into the Alamo to help its defenders. Travis sent more messages pleading for assistance, but no more help arrived.

While the Alamo lay surrounded and almost helpless, delegates previously elected by Texas voters quickly and noisily prepared a Texas declaration of independence. They were meeting in an unfinished frame building at a town called Washington-on-the-Brazos, 150 miles northeast of San Antonio.

Rumors of destruction of the Alamo kept the delegates on edge. In that day of slow communication they didn't know exactly what was happening in San Antonio.

The men besieged inside the Alamo knew. Mexican artillery pounded their fortress frequently but they shot back. Then, when ammunition in the Alamo began running low, they often held their fire. A noisy rattle from small weapons sometimes broke that silence.

Nights brought little relief from the sounds of battle. A series of distant bugle calls, shouts, and shots kept the men inside the Alamo on edge,

Tom Jones

wondering when the all-out attack would come. They knew it would come, because they had vowed not to surrender.

They had told Santa Anna this. Now, during daylight hours, a blood-red flag visible in the tower of San Fernando Church not far away served as a continual reminder of Santa Anna's announced intention of taking no prisoners from the Alamo.

The all-out attack came early in the morning of March 6, 1836, while darkness hid the movement of Mexican soldiers. Shortly after 5 A.M. they were positioned and ready. Dawn had begun showing its light. "Viva Santa Anna!" came a shout. Then came the sound of a bugle. Its call was echoed by other bugles all around the Alamo. Mexican soldiers stormed the walls from all sides.

Atop one of those walls, an Alamo officer on watch heard the bugles and quickly guessed this wasn't just another false alarm. He yelled over and over, "The Mexicans are coming!"

Weary defenders sprang to their feet, seized weapons, and ran to their positions. A din of cannon and rifle fire filled everyone's ears, but occasionally there could also be heard cheers, shouts, and screams.

Bodies of Mexican soldiers and bits and pieces of broken ladders began to clutter areas just outside the walls. The soldiers had tried to scale the walls with the ladders, but defenders firing downward from those same walls had fought them off.

The Mexicans kept coming. They succeeded in getting over the walls and into the Alamo compound. Defenders fought them from building to building and room to room, sometimes using empty rifles as clubs.

But sometimes, also, a man tried to surrender. A Mexican officer later remembered seeing a defender waving a white sock tied to his rifle. The defender didn't live to tell about it, even supposing he would have wanted to.

An hour and a half after the first bugle had sounded, the Alamo had fallen. At least 183 of its defenders died. This included every man who had fought for it. Some other persons inside the fortress survived. This included a mother and her fifteen-month-old daughter. Estimates of the Mexican dead ranged as high as fifteen hundred.

Word of the Alamo defeat spread throughout the settled portion of Texas. Most rebelling colonists fled eastward, toward the safety of the United States border. Even the main Texas army of several hundred men under General Sam Houston headed in that direction. Later this rush toward safety became known as the Runaway Scrape.

Two weeks after the loss of the Alamo, another tragedy struck the Texans fighting for freedom. At Goliad, eighty miles southeast of San Antonio, Colonel James Fannin tried to move his four hundred soldiers eastward, too, on the orders of General Sam Houston. But Fannin and his men were encircled by a large Mexican force and forced to surrender.

On March 27 the prisoners were executed, as ordered by Santa Anna. A total of 342 men died, including Fannin.

The situation looked bleak indeed for Texas independence. But suddenly everything changed.

General Santa Anna and part of his large army were chasing Sam Houston and the last remaining Texas force. Then Santa Anna blundered into an exposed position in a land he didn't know well. Marshland and water cut off several areas of possible retreat.

On this low plain near what is now the city of Houston, Santa Anna ordered a halt. The Mexicans were there, at what is known today as the San Jacinto battlefield, on April 21, 1836. That afternoon the Mexican general and many of his twelve hundred men enjoyed an afternoon nap — a siesta. They dozed even though they knew that Sam Houston and his army (918 men) had halted not far away.

About 3:30 that afternoon Houston sent his angry men into the Mexican camp for vengeance. Many of them yelled, "Remember the Alamo," as they pressed forward, firing and clubbing.

General Houston's report later said that a Texas victory came in "about eighteen minutes." Two of his men had been killed, twenty-three wounded. "The enemy's loss was 630 killed," he added. Santa Anna himself became a prisoner of the rebels.

Texas won its independence from Mexico that April afternoon 150 years ago.

TOM JONES

PART 2:
INDEPENDENCE

Victory at the Battle of San Jacinto on April 21, 1836, brought Texas a period of peace with Mexico. It also resulted in founding the Republic of Texas by people who then preferred to call themselves "Texians."

This meant that Texas would be a separate nation like Mexico itself, and like France, Spain, England, and other countries. It would not be just another state in the United States — not for a while, anyway.

The flag of the Republic of Texas became the

THE LITTLE SPANIARD
FAMED COMANCHE WARRIOR

TOM JONES
AFTER
CATLIN

fourth of those six flags that would fly over Texas. Later it would fly especially proudly over the Alamo, the symbol of Texas freedom.

But the Indian tribes that had settled in Texas long before the appearance of the first white men and women refused to agree that they should make way for the newcomers. Those natives realized very quickly that immigrants to Texas were threatening Indian life, and they fought back.

One notable fight occurred in May, 1836, at a family fort built two miles north of what is now Groesbeck, Texas, in Limestone County. An immigrant from Illinois named John Parker had brought a large number of relatives with him to the new country of Texas. Working together, they had built a spacious refuge from raiding Indians. They called it Parker's Fort.

The fort stood atop a small hill overlooking the wooded valley of the Navasota River. Every day members of the Parker family would leave the fort and work their crops, which grew in the rich soil outside the walls.

This land lay far away from the safety of other settlements, but the fields that were farmed offered the advantage of great fertility. Besides, during daylight hours the people could see any raiding Indians in the vicinity, probably before the natives could inflict much damage. The Parkers hoped this would be true, anyway.

Before nightfall the men and women who

tended the fields during daylight hours would
return to the safety of the fort and the thick log
walls that surrounded it. If they had let their horses and cattle outside the walls that morning to
graze, they would drive the animals back inside the
fort for safety, too.

After that, the people could close and lock
the large gate that allowed entrance into the fort.

Then they could relax. Two tall watchtowers built inside the fort provided a good and safe view of the area outside.

Inside, fires flickered in growing darkness just outside the log cabins that were built within the walls. The families prepared their meals over these fires. Then, after food had been eaten and the last chores had been completed, the occupants bedded down for the night in their comfortable cabins. The sturdy walls of the fort would keep out late-evening prowlers. With the gate closed, only the dim light from the starry heavens could gain entrance.

But people usually grow careless after a while if their safety measures seem needless. This happened to members of the Parker family. Sometimes they neglected to close the gate.

Early on the warm, sunny morning of Thursday, May 19, 1836, some men left the fort to work in the fields. They left the gate open behind them. No doubt it seemed to them a waste of time to close it at that bright hour.

About nine o'clock that morning a child playing inside the fort glanced out the entrance. He saw a throng of mounted Indians staring back at him from a distance.

The boy screamed. Adults still left inside the fort came running. The sight surely proved chilling to them, too.

They saw an estimated five hundred Indians

staring at the open entrance. Many of the natives obviously were Comanches, who were especially dreaded by whites living on the frontier.

Comanche Indians had long before seized numbers of horses that Spaniards like Coronado had brought from Spain. The Comanches had become skillful riders of these imported animals, and they were furious fighters. Now entirely too many of them were glaring at the fort built by the Parker family.

But the Indians offered a ray of hope — or at least they seemed to do so. The white people staring from inside the fort saw that the natives were showing a white flag, which meant they wanted to talk peace- fully. One of the Parkers, a man whose first name was Benjamin, walked out to them.

The people might have quickly shut the gate instead. But that surely would have angered the Indians. Then the Parker kinfolk already working in fields nearby would have been in great danger without knowing about it.

Benjamin Parker talked with the Indians briefly and returned to the fort. He said the Indians were claiming to be friendly. All they wanted, he said, was a supply of beef and directions to the nearest water hole.

But their request for directions to water gave away the real reason for their sudden presence at Parker's Fort. Not far away lay the Navasota River. The Indians certainly knew that fact.

Benjamin Parker told the others inside the fort he intended to return to the waiting Indians and talk further with them. He said he hoped he could prevent the attack that appeared to be coming.

Other family members pleaded with him not

to go back. Despite their appeals, Benjamin Parker once again strode out to talk with the waiting, staring, glaring Indians.

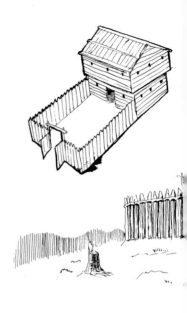

The natives were finished talking. They swarmed over Parker and killed him, while horrified relatives watched. Then the Indians rode into the fort, screeching and shouting. They ran down the occupants and killed most of them. After that they chased the people working in the fields. Some of those whites hid and later escaped.

Parker's Fort soon fell into ruin after that. Today a replica stands on the site. But the tragedy of May 19, 1836, became famous in Texas history. Details were to be remembered for years afterward because of a surprise ending to the story.

One member of the Parker family captured by the Indians was a nine-year-old girl named Cynthia Ann Parker. The Comanches took her with them, and she grew up like an Indian.

Later she married a Comanche chief, and they had children. One son, named Quanah, grew up to become the last great chief of the Comanche Indians before he and other members of the tribe were

TUMLINSON'S BLOCKHOUSE

CONJECTURAL

herded onto a reservation by the United States Army.

Earlier, during all those years of Cynthia Ann Parker's captivity, Texans had looked for her. Finally, in 1860, a group of mounted Texas Rangers who were protecting frontier settlers recaptured her during a fight with Indians.

At first Cynthia Ann Parker went unrecognized by her most recent captors. By that time she was thirty-four years old, and she looked exactly like an Indian except for one difference. She had blue eyes. This difference helped identify her.

Captured with Cynthia Ann Parker was her two-year-old daughter, Prairie Flower. Cynthia Ann asked the Rangers to allow her and her daughter to return to the only life they knew — life with the Comanches. But the men who had "saved" her from the Indians insisted on sending her and Prairie Flower to live with surviving members of the Parker family in East Texas. In only a few years Cynthia Ann and her daughter both died there.

But the story didn't end even there. The Comanche chief named Quanah, son of Cynthia Ann, took his mother's last name. As Quanah Parker he became the father of children. Today, members of the Parker family gather for summer reunions — often at the replica of Parker's Fort. Approximately half of those Parkers are white. The rest are at least part Indian. Their long story serves as a continuing reminder of those days of the vanished Republic of Texas.

The earliest days of Texas independence proved to be hard — not easy at all. The new republic had little money. Mexico refused to admit that a Republic of Texas existed. At first, not even the United States helped much.

Texans had been counting on aid from the United States. Most citizens of the Lone Star republic wanted Texas to become a state as soon as possible. That would solve many problems.

But the United States government had problems of its own. Slavery, which existed then,

had begun to cause a serious division in the country. Southern states allowed slavery and wanted it to continue. Northern states insisted on doing away with slavery throughout the United States.

In Texas in those years slavery was legal. Many Americans opposed letting Texas in the Union for that reason.

So Texas remained outside the United States. Some Texas leaders desired this. They dreamed of an emerging empire that they, themselves, would lead to greatness in the world. Actually, however, the Texas republic seemed more like a story out of

comic opera. Here are some facts that made the idea of a Texas empire a funny thought indeed:

Texas claimed as part of its area a large chunk of land that included parts of what are now New Mexico, Oklahoma, Kansas, Colorado, and Wyoming (as well as Texas, of course). But officials of the young republic were not even able to govern very well the settled parts of East Texas and the Gulf Coast — let alone the other large territories.

The official residence of the first president of Texas was sometimes called the "Executive Mansion." That's the same name given the White House home of the United States president. But the Republic of Texas "Executive Mansion" was nothing more than a crude, double log cabin. Its first occupant —who was also the first elected president of Texas, Sam Houston — sometimes surprised visitors to the poor log "mansion" by dressing in a velvet coat and trousers trimmed with broad gold lace.

The next president of Texas, who was a man with the impressive name of Mirabeau Buonaparte Lamar, was one of those men who saw greatness ahead for the Texas republic. But Lamar also imagined a great treasury to match. He nearly destroyed the young nation by spending too freely in an effort to make his Texas dreams come true.

Meanwhile, President Lamar had won recognition of Texas independence by the French gov-

SAM HOUSTON

st. PRESIDENT   REPUBLIC of TEXAS

MIRABEAU LAMAR

2ND. PRESIDENT   REPUBLIC OF TEX

ernment. This had not been easy to do. However, Texas' friendship with France was endangered for a time by some pigs that roamed areas of Austin near the French Embassy. The incident became known as the "Pig War."

The "war" began when the French envoy to Texas complained that pigs belonging to an Austin man were misbehaving badly. The animals had invaded horse stables on the grounds of the French Embassy and had eaten fodder intended for those horses.

The same pigs had even managed to work their way into the Frenchman's bedroom. There they had eaten some of the linen and chewed on embassy papers.

The government of Texas was slow to act on the Frenchman's complaint. So the angry envoy left Austin without even telling his own government in Paris until later. For a time relations between Texas and France were broken off.

Three things helped to keep Texas a republic for ten years.

First, the election of Sam Houston as Texas president helped greatly. Some citizens disliked and even hated Sam Houston. But the old hero of the Battle of San Jacinto was possibly the only man capable of keeping the weak, new republic together during his two terms of office.

Second, the hard work of some other Texans

who believed in the future greatness of their country helped keep it going.

Third, and probably most important, the Republic of Texas owed its life to weakness and conflict that divided Mexico during these years. The Mexican government tried several times to bring down the new republic. Mexico sought to incite Texas Indians into open warfare against white settlers. Mexico also sent several military expeditions into Texas. But Texas never was reconquered.

Sam Houston helped there, too. Houston knew that spending large amounts of money, even for military defense, would ruin his country.

He cut government spending. He also refused to be swept into a war favored by many Texas citizens who became angry about the occasional brief invasions from Mexico.

Life during the early days of the Republic of Texas actually wasn't much easier than it had been earlier, before independence. Every village in the

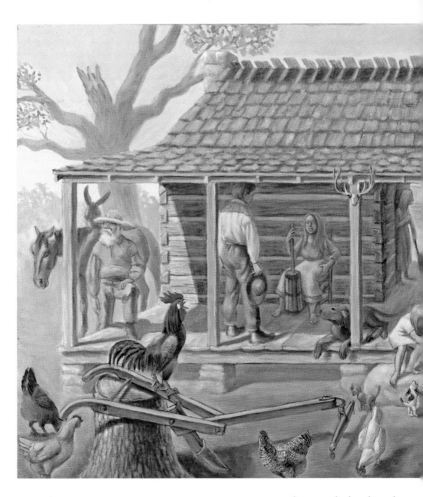

settled area of Texas was new and crudely built, with the exception of three old towns — San Antonio, Nacogdoches, and Goliad. The newly built villages were only shabby collections of log cabins and sheds built along dirt streets that became dusty during dry spells and muddy during wet weather. Stumps left from recently cut trees cluttered some streets, making walking or riding at night hazardous.

The Texas of that long-ago time was largely a man's world. It was a hard place of hard toil relieved only occasionally by rough play. Most men chewed and spat tobacco. When they had time to sit and talk, they would often take out a pocket knife and whittle on some piece of wood found nearby.

They often drank too much liquor, especially on election days, holidays, and Sundays. Drinking

Tom Jones

almost always made the independent-minded, argument-prone men even more quarrelsome. That led to further uproar.

"In this vile community," one man wrote, "a boxing match is the prettiest way in the world of settling a difficulty... Chivalry has not yet found entrance in Texas."

Fewer women than men had "found entrance" into Texas, too. That's one reason early Texas was such a rough place. The women who *had* come to Texas were mostly individuals of great mental strength, reliability, and ability to make-do with the few household goods they found available. Those women had to be that way to survive at such a hard time in Texas history. For that reason they played an important part in the development of Texas.

Despite the scarcity of women, dancing was a favorite recreation in Texas — along with drinking and fighting, and horse racing. Word of a coming dance spread quickly around the countryside, especially among females of any age. Dancing partners for men sometimes included girls not yet in their teens.

Dance steps popular then told something about the rough times. The steps danced most often were shuffles and stomps — not smooth glides, which were impossible to perform on dirt or split-log floors.

Even harder to find than female dancing partners were good doctors. And even when they could be found, the medicine they practiced in that day was crude compared to today's treatment.

Fevers raged in river bottoms and other stagnant areas along the low-lying Gulf Coast. Sickness became especially bad during the summers, when the heat soared to heights that probably caused some immigrants to long for the bitter-cold winters they had left behind somewhere.

During the hot spells, epidemics occasionally raged. An inability to keep food chilled and an absence of sanitation brought on many sicknesses, such as cholera and dysentery. Newcomers often fell quick victims to malaria or yellow fever, especially in the summer.

Doctors of those old days relied on quinine, calomel, and patent medicines to cure their patients. Another treatment thought to be effective was drawing blood from an ill person. Surviving any sickness was a continual worry for those early Texans.

Difficult, too, was travel — and sometimes it was impossible during or after heavy rains that turned normally dusty roads into a sort of brown squash and sent streams rampaging out of their banks. Partly because of these troubles mail service was very poor during days of the republic.

But advances came in other ways. The United

States finally recognized Texas independence — on March 3, 1837, one year after the delegates at Washington-on-the-Brazos had signed the declaration. This meant the United States would deal with Texas as a free nation, the same as Mexico, France, England, and those other countries.

Sam Houston was president when that happened. But President Lamar, who served just after Houston, can be thanked for helping with other progress.

It was Lamar who officially approved the "Lone Star" flag for use by the republic, in January, 1839. This is now the state flag.

Lamar also began planning for what would become the public school system in Texas, though it was years before free education became available to all children.

It was also Lamar who proposed Austin as the capital of Texas. He had been impressed by the beauty of the place even before he became president.

During the autumn of 1838 Lamar and some other men were hunting buffalo near a small village named Waterloo. Lamar was said to have killed a bull while racing his horse along what is now Austin's Congress Avenue, heading toward the Colorado River.

Later the hunting party relaxed on a hill overlooking the lonely site — the hill where the Texas

Capitol now stands. Lamar looked around and remarked that the hill would be a good choice as "the seat of future Empire."

So it was that many things President Lamar did helped Texas. But some other Lamar policies probably did more harm than good.

He fought offensive wars against Indians. He forced the Cherokees out of Texas, despite earlier promises of peace given them by other white Texans.

He spent those large sums of money on Texas military forces. This included a Texas Navy, which occasionally fought Mexican warships on the Gulf of Mexico.

He organized and sent a large and costly "Santa Fe Expedition" to New Mexico, a land that Texas claimed at that time. Lamar's purpose was to bring New Mexico under Texas control and to get profits for his republic from trading with people there.

His plan failed. The expedition, attacked by Mexican soldiers, proved to be a disaster.

When Sam Houston was elected president for a second term, in 1841, he took Lamar's place and tried to undo some things Lamar had done.

Houston cut government spending. He tried to disband the Texas Navy. He moved the Texas government out of Austin — first to Houston, then to Washington-on-the-Brazos. But when his men tried to move valuable government papers, called archives, out of Austin for safekeeping, angry residents of that city stopped them. The residents were led by a woman who directed the aiming and firing of eight cannon shots. That dispute became known as the "Archive War."

Sam Houston's men gave up their attempt. The papers stayed in Austin, and they were there when the Texas government returned a few years later.

President Houston's largest problem probably was trying to keep his angry countrymen from seeking revenge every time a Mexican force raided into Texas. Houston was sure that renewed warfare could only hurt Texas chances for survival. But

many Texans wondered if the one-time victor of San Jacinto hadn't turned into a coward.

Finally, public pressure forced Sam Houston to retaliate after one Mexican raid into San Antonio. Further angering Texas citizens was the fact that their old enemy, General Santa Anna, had returned to power in Mexico and was responsible for much of the trouble.

So, late in 1842, Houston approved sending a Texas army of militia and volunteers on a raid into Mexico. But he did this half-heartedly, and he told the commander of the force to return home if failure seemed likely.

The expedition did indeed break up, but not

all members returned home. About three hundred of the soldiers wanted to invade Mexico. They elected their own commander to lead them on. Their group became known as the "Mier Expedition." It ended tragically for them.

The men attacked the Mexican town of Mier, but they were forced to surrender. They were being marched deep into Mexico to be put in prison when, at sunrise one morning, they overpowered their guards in a courtyard where they were being held overnight. They escaped, but most of them were recaptured in a few weeks.

Just before sunset on March 25, 1843, these Texas prisoners were herded into the same courtyard from which they had escaped earlier. The

T.S. SAN ANTONIO — T.S. SAN BERNARD — TOPSAIL SCHOONERS — T.S. SAN JACINTO — T.S. ZAVALA — STEAM SHIP OF WAR

Texans — 176 in all, bound in pairs — no longer had any ability even to try another escape, as their sickly appearance showed. But this time they were heavily guarded by alert soldiers who surely intended to give them no chance to break out again.

A colorfully uniformed officer appeared and read an order from General Santa Anna. Every tenth Texan present would be executed. The prisoners heard the sentence read with "inexpressible horror," one of them said later.

Santa Anna originally had ordered death for every prisoner. But the governor of the Mexican state where the Texans were being held refused to obey this order. In Mexico City, other people objected to Santa Anna's demand. Finally, the

original order was changed. One of every ten prisoners would die.

The officer explained how it would be decided who should die and who should live. Seventeen black beans and 159 white beans would be poured into a clay jar, which would then be shaken. Each prisoner would draw a bean. Black meant death. White meant life.

When the jar was ready the officer held it far above his head — so high the prisoners couldn't see into it. Then each of them drew a bean.

Survivors said later that not one man — not even one who had drawn a black bean — allowed his captors to see whatever terror filled his soul. One man who was awarded death in this awful lottery even joked about it. He held up the black bean between his thumb and forefinger and said, "Boys, I told you so; I never failed in my life to draw a prize."

Such misery wasn't necessarily enjoyed by the captors. As is usual in war, they were military men following orders given by someone else. Several Mexican officers who presided at the grim twilight ceremony wept. When the seventeen losers were executed by rifle fire, a Mexican sentry standing atop a wall was so sickened by the sight that he swayed dizzily and nearly fell off.

After the executions, the other 159 prisoners were taken on into Mexico, to a prison south of Mexico City named Perote. Eventually the last Texas prisoner held there was released on September 16, 1844 — by none other than General Santa Anna.

At that time Sam Houston was still president of Texas. But two weeks earlier Texans had elected the man who would take Houston's place. The new president was to be Anson Jones, a native of Massachusetts who had become a doctor of medicine before moving to Texas in 1833.

Sam Houston spent much of his last year as president in working to get Texas accepted as a state by the United States. But Americans who

opposed slavery continued to keep Texas out of the Union.

Then Houston and other Texas officials tried something else. They decided to worry the United States into accepting Texas.

Republic of Texas officials suddenly became very friendly with certain European countries —

especially with England. That did indeed worry government authorities in Washington, D.C. The United States had won its own independence, of course, from England about seventy years earlier. Since then the United States and England had fought still another war and had been engaged in other disputes resulting from English presence in North America. Now those same Americans were wondering what England might be planning with the Republic of Texas.

That resulted in annexation of Texas as a state by the United States Congress and president. The date this officially occurred was December 29, 1845. But the final transfer of authority from republic to state was made almost two months later, on February 19, 1846.

Many Texans thought their troubles were over. One woman wrote in her diary, "Thank God we are now annexed to the U. States and can hope for home and quiet." But even while she wrote that, United States Army troops commanded by General Zachary Taylor prepared to march from Corpus Christi to the Mexican border. The troops had

been ordered into Texas by United States President James K. Polk. They were prepared to defend the new state against attack by Mexico, which had been angered by the United States takeover of Texas. Mexico never had admitted that Texas was truly an independent country.

On that day when the Republic of Texas passed into history, a ceremony in Austin was held to mark the occasion. At noon cannon boomed a salute. Atop a pole the United States flag replaced that of the republic. And the last president of Texas, Anson Jones, said with emotion that brought tears to the eyes of some listeners, "The Republic of Texas is no more."

PART 3:
THE FRONTIER

Annexation in 1845 meant that Texas would no longer be a poor, struggling republic. Now it would be a poor, struggling state in the United States. The United States flag was the fifth one to fly over Texas.

The poorness and the struggle could be easily seen by looking around the capital "city" of Austin. In those years its population numbered fewer than one thousand residents. In fact, the estimated

population of the entire state of Texas in 1845 just about equaled the number of 1980 residents — 149,230 — counted by only one city, Amarillo. But in 1845 Amarillo didn't even exist.

Austin barely existed, it seemed. It had been founded only six years earlier, after Mirabeau

Buonaparte Lamar had promoted it as "the seat of future Empire." But when Texas became a state, Austin possibly seemed more like the seat of some badly worn, patched trousers.

Frame buildings lined both sides of Congress Avenue, the street that runs southward from the hill where the Capitol building now stands. During those years, heavy rains would turn unpaved Congress Avenue into a long puddle of mud.

But most boosters of Austin could overlook that hardship. About this time one resident used his imagination to look far beyond the Congress Avenue mud, and he wrote, "The city of Austin bids fair to become one of the most refined and pleasant cities in the western world."

Many of the crude, wood-frame buildings of downtown Austin gave off a country smell of new lumber — something rarely smelled downtown anywhere these days of the 1980's.

All the government buildings were made of wood. For several years even the one-story Capitol building was wooden.

But the countryside near Austin was impressive, as Lamar had seen. From the fertile, meadow-like valley of the Colorado River, the land nearby rose in gentle swells.

To the northwest some steep, tree-covered hills looked down on the river. For several years after the founding of Austin these wooded hills had been inhabited by Indians who sometimes

SATANTA

swooped down on the new town in quick raids. The exposed location of Austin had been a big reason that Sam Houston didn't approve of the choice of that town as the Texas capital.

By 1845, however, the area was safer. Austin residents had become fond of taking picnic dinners to the top of one of those steep hills, called Mount Bonnell. It is still a landmark today.

Throughout the countryside around Austin a thirsty man or woman could find cool, clear springs and streams. One newcomer wrote that the general appearance was "of as healthy a country as I ever saw." A few residents suffered from agues and fevers, but Austin generally escaped the sicknesses that plagued lowlands along the Gulf Coast.

Many other parts of what is now the state of Texas were largely unknown in 1845 — and some

areas hadn't even been seen except through Indian eyes.

Much of the high plains country of the Texas Panhandle was known only to Indians. That region — an elevated, treeless flatland — received enough rainfall so that plentiful grass grew. But it also had cold winters for such a moderate latitude.

A few hundred miles southwest of the plains lay a much different landscape. There, in the area of Texas known today as the Big Bend, barren mountains rose skyward. Later, map-makers would count ninety peaks that towered above a mile in height in far west Texas. One of them, Guadalupe Peak, rose more than a mile and a half into the heavens. This is known today as the highest point in Texas — 8,751 feet. But in those days Indians controlled most of that country, too.

West of Austin lay a rolling, wooded "hill country," as it is called today. During the early days of Texas statehood, more and more settlers began moving into it, but not without meeting some angry Indians.

Another area that had been slow to attract settlers was a wide strip of coastal land lying between what are now the cities of Corpus Christi and Brownsville. There, in a dry, prickly country of scrubby trees and short grass or none at all, sunshine of long summers baked the land. Even today, that region contains fewer residents than most other parts of Texas. But some important, wealthy ranchers own large sections of land there now.

Southward from that dry area of scrubby trees, and lying along the banks of the Rio Grande, were settlements that had existed for many years. Settlers in that region were Mexican. Far northward up the river, near where El Paso stands today, a town named Ysleta became known as the oldest permanent settlement in Texas. The town grew up around a Spanish mission built in 1681.

But the eastern part of Texas was, of course, best known to settlers from the United States. Many trees found there had to be cut down before farmers could till the soil. However, the usually plentiful rainfall then brought crops to a good harvest.

So, that year of 1845, the United States formally took over all these Texas lands, good and

TOM JONES

bad, forested and barren, wet and dry, smooth and rugged. Under its new, eager, westward-looking administrators, all of Texas would be thoroughly known before long.

The United States had already moved to protect its newest state against further Mexican attack. General Zachary Taylor and 3,900 United States Army soldiers had encamped at Corpus Christi Bay, ready to fight Mexico for Texas.

As long as Taylor's army held that position, an attack by Mexico was unlikely. Mexico never had given up its claim to any part of Texas, but at least General Taylor and his men were staying within the historic borders of that disputed state by camping at Corpus Christi Bay. They were remaining near the Nueces River, which had been considered the boundary of Texas since the days when Spain claimed the whole area.

But if Taylor's army marched farther south and westward — into that dry, prickly country of scrubby trees and short grass between the Nueces and the Rio Grande— Mexico surely would consider it the same as a declaration of war. Mexico claimed ownership of the land on both sides of the Rio Grande, toward which Taylor seemed ready to march. Only the old Republic of Texas, and then the United States, considered the Rio Grande as being the border between Texas and Mexico.

Orders from United States President James K. Polk did indeed arrive, sending Taylor's army to the Rio Grande. In Washington, D.C., many of Polk's opponents accused him of wanting to start a war to take Mexican territory. Some Americans and many Mexicans still believe that was Polk's purpose. Whatever the reason for the orders, General Taylor carried them out. He had indicated to some friends he opposed angering Mexico by making such a move. But in the end Taylor was, after all, a professional military man, and President Polk was his commander.

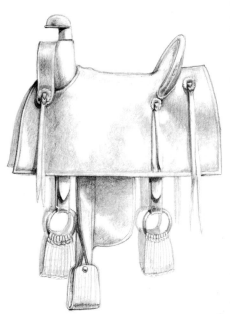

The march to the Rio Grande began at ten o'clock Sunday morning, March 8, 1846, across a country in the bloom of a South Texas spring. Mounted soldiers called dragoons — 378 of them — clomped out first. They were followed by creaking supply wagons and by rumbling horse-drawn guns of Taylor's artillery.

With the artillery rode a young lieutenant named Sam French, a native of New Jersey and a recent graduate of the United States Military Academy. French was happy to be in Texas and now was excited to be on his way toward Mexico. He wanted "to know the world by sight and not by books," as he wrote once.

But French's happiness dimmed a little with every hour that passed on the march. Rain had wet the countryside and had brought forth a spring-like display of "blue flowers like the hyacinth" — probably the Texas bluebonnet. But beneath the flowers and grass and weeds lurked rattlesnakes. When the unit halted for the night, French looked around and saw soldiers standing beside grazing army animals and some-times hitting at rattlers with long sticks cut for that purpose.

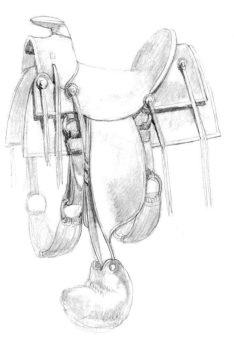

During the march toward Mexico, sun and wind brought further discomfort. That combination of climate burned many lips and noses. Sometimes lips became so raw that men couldn't stand touching them to tin cups filled with hot coffee. Instead they waited for the drink to cool.

Young Lieutenant Sam French fared a little better. During the day he wore a huge Mexican sombrero, despite the warnings of other officers who told him that General Taylor would probably be angry if he should see one of his lieutenants so clearly out of uniform. But when the sombrero-shaded French finally came across Taylor, he was relieved to hear the General say, "Good morning, Lieutenant, good morning. Sensible man to wear a hat."

The rest of General Taylor's forces began leaving Corpus Christi Bay for Mexico on the morning of March 9. They left in three large groups, called "brigades," March 9, 10, and 11.

The men of Taylor's army averaged ten miles a day during the march to Mexico. They traveled two hundred winding miles — through rain, then across sun-baked soil, through suffocating dust, past occasional holes of brackish or salt water, and

through ankle-deep sand that burned like hot ashes.

Near the Rio Grande the landscape began to change for the better. Grass thickened. Trees and flowers reappeared. But rumors of attack by Mexican soldiers began to spread among Taylor's men.

No battle came, however, and late in the morning of March 28, 1846, Taylor's army neared its goal. Sam French, the young lieutenant who wanted "to know the world by sight," and others saw the mud-colored Rio Grande ahead of them. Its waters, two hundred yards wide, swept between steep banks toward the Gulf of Mexico.

French and the others saw, on the other side of the river, the Mexican town of Matamoros. It was a town of white houses built amid tropical gardens. The scene appeared "like a fairy vision" before the staring soldiers. The long, unpleasant march apparently had been worth it.

General Taylor ordered his men to dig in at this site. They built "Fort Texas" protected originally by dirt walls. Later the name was changed to Fort Brown. Some of its old buildings can still be seen at Brownsville, the city that grew up around it.

After a few weeks, fighting broke out. A Mexican force crossed the Rio Grande and fired on a patrol of American soldiers. Since the attack came on the northeast side of the river — land claimed by the United States — General Taylor sent a message to President Polk saying, "Hostilities may now be considered as commenced." What the General meant was that war had started.

Taylor's message took two weeks to reach Washington, D.C., because of the poor communications and slow travel of that day. Congress, pressed by President Polk, officially declared war on Mexico.

The first two battles of the United States' war against Mexico were fought on Texas soil. Both battles occurred in the vicinity of today's Brownsville. After that, the fighting moved into Mexico.

The man who had only recently been elected the first governor of Texas, James Pinckney Henderson, left his office in charge of Lieutenant Governor Albert C. Horton. Then Henderson set out to fight in Mexico as a major general commanding an army of Texas volunteers. More than eight thousand Texans served with United States forces.

Among the Texans were numbers of Texas Rangers, called by many Mexicans *los diablos Tejanos*. In English, this meant "the Texas devils."

The Rangers were still remembering the Alamo. In addition to that, the Rangers were again fighting General Santa Anna, the old enemy of

Texas. Santa Anna had returned to power yet another time after falling out of favor there for a while.

A colonel in the United States Army watched a regiment of Texas Rangers riding into Mexico City after that city had surrendered. He wrote this description:

"[Jack] Hays's rangers have come — their appearance never to be forgotten. Not in any sort of uniform, but well mounted and doubly armed: each man has one or two Colt's revolvers besides ordinary pistols, a sword, and every man his rifle. All sorts of coats, blankets, and headgear, but they are strong athletic fellows. The Mexicans are terribly afraid of them." Most of the Rangers wore long beards, which contributed to a savage appearance.

The Mexican War ended with a peace treaty signed in February, 1848. The United States won from Mexico a vast western region that stretched to the Pacific Coast. It included land that would become the states of New Mexico, Arizona, California, Nevada, and Utah — as well as large parts of Wyoming and Colorado. Mexico also gave up any claim to Texas, and agreed to set the boundary at the Rio Grande. In return, the United States paid Mexico fifteen million dollars.

Texans still were not finished with fighting. Although the war against Mexico had ended, there was more trouble ahead. Slavery continued to divide the United States.

Texas had come into the Union as a state that allowed slavery, and most Texans in those days wanted to keep it that way. But not *every* Texan agreed.

One day long ago an old black woman — a former slave — who lived in Marlin, Texas, told about her experience of being sold.

She had been brought by ship from Africa to

New Orleans. There she and other blacks were chained and displayed before a crowd of buyers. The buyers examined the blacks as if they were just so many cattle.

A plantation owner named Jones, from Fayette County, Texas, bought the woman and some other slaves. He left them in the care of an assistant, called an "overseer," and returned home.

The overseer, "a white man named Smith," soon showed himself to be the meanest man the black woman had ever known. He chained all the slaves together and took them to La Grange, Texas. Whatever one slave did, they all had to do. If one drank out of a stream, they all drank. When a slave became tired or sick while walking, the others were forced to drag or carry the sufferer.

MAS MURPHREE HOUSE
1848 as the center of a large cattle
omaston Vicinity~DeWitt County.

TOM JONES

But the plantation owner was a more gentle man. Besides that, the slaves were his property — the same as money in a bank. "Marse" Jones noticed the condition of his slaves when they arrived at the plantation. He scolded his overseer, called for a doctor to treat the blacks, then allowed them to rest for several days before putting them to work on his farm.

In spite of the widespread disagreement over slavery, Texas made some progress during the 1850's.

Its boundary was

finally settled. On maps Texas began looking as it does today.

The state's permanent school fund got its first money — two million dollars.

Travel and transportation began to improve, mainly because of railroad construction. Stagecoach lines were expanded. Steamboats navigated

some rivers. About this time the United States Army experimented with the use of imported camels for carrying supplies to military posts in the desert Southwest. The experiment failed.

But those newly built army posts helped to protect settlers along the western and northwest-

ern frontiers. Still, hostile Indians remained a danger there.

Immigration into Texas from both Europe and the United States increased. Many Germans founded busy, neatly kept towns, especially in Central Texas. But other people arrived, too, and

contributed to Texas society: Jews, Poles, Czechs, Italians, Frenchmen, Greeks, Scandinavians, and others.

In 1860 three-fourths of the people in Texas had been born outside the state — and many had been born outside the United States. Texans showed these differences. But their way of life in those hard frontier days made them the same, too,

in many ways. Most Texans — men and women and even older children — were rugged, independent (yet quick to help a neighbor in need), self-reliant, and proud of their abilities.

Most Texans lived on farms. Even the towns were very small then, compared to today's cities. Most money came from farming — from cotton and corn crops. But most farmers worked hard and earned only little cash, as has been true often throughout history.

In 1859 the general who had led Texas to the San Jacinto victory, Sam Houston, was elected governor. A showdown between northern and southern states was near.

Houston tried to persuade Texans to remain in the Union, but he failed. In 1861 Texas citizens voted to leave the United States, after trying so hard for years to get into it. Texas joined other southern, slave-holding states in a government called the Confederate States of America. The flag of that Confederacy became the sixth flag to fly over Texas.

Houston resigned as governor rather than take an oath of allegiance to the new government. But he warned Texans that the United States government under newly elected President Abraham Lincoln would not allow a break-up of the Union. United States military and naval forces would be sent south, Houston said, and the southern states would be subdued. Houston added that the war

would be bloody, and that it would leave Texas and the entire South in ruins.

Time proved Houston right. Not much of the Civil War fighting took place in Texas. But thousands of Texas men and boys joined the Confederate army and fought in other states. Many of them never returned to Texas. Both armies suffered huge losses. The conflict was much worse than the Mexican War.

The people who stayed in Texas during the Civil War suffered plenty of hardship — from a scarcity of food, clothing, and other necessities of life. Diaries, journals, and letters left behind by people who lived then tell of their troubles.

Real coffee became scarce when Union warships blockaded towns on the Gulf and stopped the shipment of supplies into Texas. People boiled parched wheat as a very poor substitute for brewed coffee. Women made over their old dresses into clothes for girls and boys. Scraps went into cheap — but lovingly fashioned — home-made dolls for Christmas gifts. Women and girls knitted shawls and mittens and stockings, then gave the things color by dying them with walnut hulls or the bark of certain trees.

Toward the end of that long and bloody Civil War, Texans could buy very few products at stores — even if the people had money. They had to get by with what they could provide with their own hands.

Finally, the war ended the way Sam Houston had said it would. The South was forced to surrender — in 1865. A Union general and eighteen hundred soldiers arrived at Galveston to take possession of Texas. On June 19 of that year the general declared that all slaves in Texas were now free men and women. He was following orders sent from Washington, D.C. Today in Texas blacks

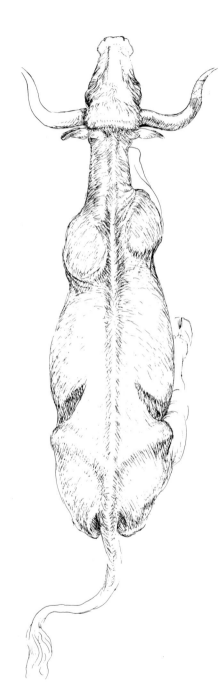

celebrate that June 19, 1865, day of freedom as "Juneteenth."

During the days and months that followed the end of the Civil War, confusion and chaos gripped Texas. Government fell apart. Bandits and burglars roamed the countryside. Eventually, however, the Union conquerors took control of the state. For several years they acted much like dictators, during a period known as "Reconstruction." They forced Texas and other defeated southern states to follow policies dictated from Washington, D.C. During this time Texas didn't have the status of a state in the United States. But in 1870 Texas was readmitted to the Union.

The period after the Civil War became famous for the rise of the Texas cattle industry. It happened this way:

Earlier, after Texas had won independence from Mexico, many Mexican ranchers moved back southward across the Rio Grande to their own country. They left behind, in Southwest Texas, numbers of Longhorn cattle that had originally come from Spain. The animals multiplied quickly.

In Texas the cattle brought little cash, especially in the hard times after the Civil War. If the animals could be sold at all, the top price was three or four dollars each. On northern markets cattle

brought ten times as much money. So Texans began driving their cattle northward, to railroad depots in Kansas or elsewhere. From there the animals could be shipped eastward.

This work made the cowboy famous in Texas history. The cattle roamed fenceless ranges. Cowboys — some of them black-skinned — rounded up the animals twice a year. So that the different owners could keep track of their cattle, the young calves were "branded" — marked with a symbol that showed which rancher owned each calf.

Ranching spread from Southwest Texas to areas in the state farther north. Texans moving onto an ever-shrinking frontier pushed the Indians back. The United States Army helped make the frontier safe. So did buffalo hunters, though the hunters didn't have that goal in mind. The hunters killed so many buffalo that the Indians were left without food and clothing that the buffalo provided.

Several years before the end of the nineteenth century, American Indians had been moved onto large sections of land called reservations. They ceased to threaten the frontier. But even before that happened, ranchers and some farmers had moved into the Texas Panhandle and into other areas of the state that hadn't been inhabited earlier.

Women rarely rode the range. One newly married lady named Mary Bunton proved to be an exception. Later she wrote about it.

Mary lived with her new husband on a ranch near Sweetwater, Texas. Even before she married him she was known as a good rider of horses. In those days she rode side-saddle — as did all ladies. On the ranch, however, she decided to wear riding pants and to sit astride the horse.

When the cowboys saw her riding this way they nearly stampeded. One old cowboy stared at

her and exclaimed, "I knew she'd do it! Here she comes wearin' the britches!"

Mary even rode with her husband on a cattle drive up the Chisholm Trail in 1886. But the invention and use of barbed-wire fences on the vast ranges soon made the long cattle drives impossible.

As the year 1899 neared its end the frontier in Texas had almost disappeared. This meant also, of course, that the nineteenth century was on its way out. Nowhere was the end of that century more noticed than at Galveston. A vicious hurricane that struck the city September 8, 1900, was responsible.

In those days Galveston had no seawall for protection. People weren't worried, however, because a strong storm hadn't struck their city in many years.

But on the morning of that September 8, 1900 — a Saturday — the force of the tide and wind kept getting stronger and stronger. Weathermen had warned Galvestonians to leave low areas, but many citizens delayed until too late. Around noon, storm-whipped water from the Gulf of Mexico had begun to swirl on the first floors of some residences, even though the buildings had been erected with first floors elevated several feet above the ground.

Sarah Littlejohn, eight years old, stayed inside her home that day because of the weather. For a while she played dolls in a room upstairs with her two sisters and a friend who was visiting her. Soon afterward she wrote an account of that day.

At noon, she said, it was raining hard. Her father came home from work. Then her friend's father came over to take his daughter home. Water hadn't yet risen into the Littlejohn residence. But Sarah could see high — and rising — water about a block away.

By mid-afternoon water in their yard was waist-deep. Sarah's mother noticed a man struggling through the water and wind, and she called to him to come inside.

"He was an old German, and we could not understand him very well . . . . It seemed to me that he could not understand us [either], for it took mamma a very long time to make him come inside.

". . . It surely did sound funny to hear him talk. He said he did not mind the water, but it was the wind he did not like. He was an old fisherman."

At eight o'clock that black night Sarah and her family were waiting out the storm in an upstairs bathroom, which seemed the safest place to be.

The old man had refused to go upstairs with them. He sat in a rocking chair downstairs, water all around him. He had propped his feet against the front door.

Suddenly the door blew open and tossed the old man across the hall. Sarah's father went downstairs to help the man close the door, but it blew open again. Finally Mr. Littlejohn found some nails and pieces of lumber. He nailed the door shut, then he rejoined his family in the bathroom upstairs.

"The ceilings were leaking badly and the water felt so cold," Sarah wrote. "We were all wet because the water was dripping down on us." Then a mighty gust of wind hit the house.

"There goes the window pane," Sarah's mother yelled. It blew out — "as quick as lightning."

Sarah thought she heard someone crying in the darkness outside, not far away. Later, when she could look, she saw the bodies of a man and a young girl in the yard. She saw also that a white cottage had drifted against the side of the Littlejohns' house.

That awful hurricane killed from five thousand to eight thousand persons in Galveston and elsewhere along the Gulf Coast. Water completely covered the ground on which Galveston — then a city with 37,000 residents — was built.

Elsewhere in the state, Texans were quietly saying goodbye to the nineteenth century. But in Galveston on that dark September 8, 1900, many people said goodbye to much more than the nineteenth century.

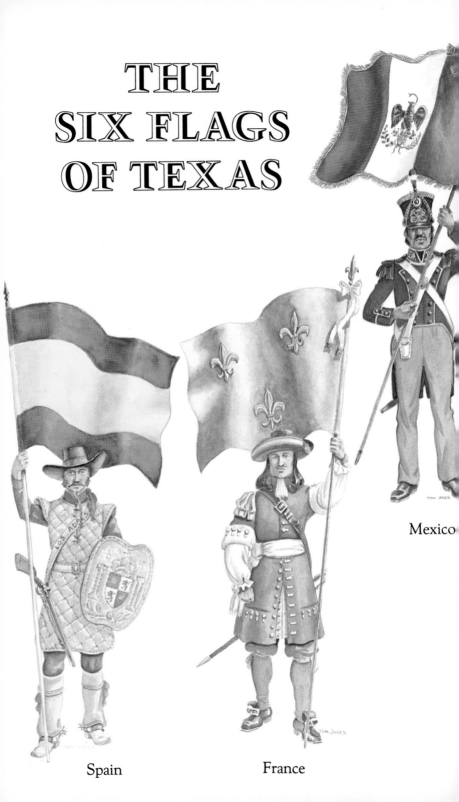

THE
SIX FLAGS
OF TEXAS

Mexico

Spain

France

Republic of Texas

United States
of America

Confederate States of America

PART 4:
THE 20TH CENTURY

On a hill four miles south of the small, quiet town of Beaumont, Texas, several members of an oil-drilling crew saw the twentieth century come in with a boom. It happened on January 10, 1901.

In the early days of the twentieth century, Beaumont had fewer than ten thousand residents. But Beaumont had a remarkable citizen whose work did much to make the town world-famous later in 1901. That citizen was largely responsible

Santa Rita No. 1

for the presence of the oil-drilling crew near Beaumont on January 10 that year.

The man's name was Pattillo Higgins. For years Higgins had taught himself geology, especially as it could be used to find oil that lay far beneath the earth's surface. And for years Higgins had told anyone who would listen that oil could be found beneath the hill that poked up from the surrounding land about four miles south of downtown Beaumont.

Higgins tried to drill for the oil himself, but he didn't have enough money for all the required work. He was forced to halt his drilling before he could prove that oil did indeed exist far below the hill. This didn't stop him from telling others that oil was to be found there.

After a while many Beaumont residents began calling Higgins "the town fool." They ignored his continued predictions about oil, except to laugh and jeer. But Higgins' ideas attracted the attention of a wealthy man who lived far from Beaumont—a man named Anthony Lucas, who lived in Washington, D.C.

Lucas listened to Beaumont's "town fool" even though Higgins' ideas about oil were different from some widely accepted beliefs. For instance, one "expert" had said earlier that he would drink all the oil that could be found west of the Mississippi River.

In those days not many oil fields had been discovered in the United States. The first large field, and the most important one of the nineteenth century, had been found in Pennsylvania in the 1850's. By 1901 oil had also been found elsewhere, including rather small quantities in East Texas.

But at that time large amounts of oil were not really needed. Automobiles had just been invented, and they were still rare. Most steamships and trains burned coal for energy. So did most factories. Oil was used then mostly for providing lighting (from oil-burning lamps, for example) and lubrication (like axle grease).

Still, many persons realized that finding oil could mean finding great riches. One such person was Anthony Lucas. He used his money to drill on the hill south of Beaumont.

The crew that was drilling that famous day in

1901 had begun the work weeks earlier. On January 10, a Thursday, the weather was clear, but cold. A strong north wind chilled the men as they worked, and it blew wood smoke from Beaumont chimneys southward. The drillers could smell the smoke.

Without warning, a giant stream of mud blew out of the hole the men had drilled. It drenched the men and sent them running for safety.

The drillers saw what amounted to six tons of four-inch pipe shoot up from the hole. The pipe flew into the air and knocked off the top of the oil derrick. Then all this wreckage crashed to the ground almost like shrapnel on a battlefield.

When calm returned, the men began creeping back to the drilling site, but they ran again when a cannon-like blast shook the area. Later, people

who lived miles away from the hill said they had heard the roar.

One member of the drilling crew, a man named Al Hamill, stared in awe as a stream of slime, then a column of blue gas, erupted from the hole they had drilled. But calm returned once more, and Hamill crept back to the hole and stared into it.

Later Hamill described what he saw: "I . . . looked down in the hole there," Hamill said. "I heard . . . something . . . bubbling . . . and looked down there, and [some] frothy oil was [bubbling upward]. It was . . . breathing-like, you know, coming up and sinking back with the gas pressure. And it kept coming up . . . and each flow a little higher and a little higher and a little higher. Finally it came up with such [force] that it just shot up clear through the top of the derrick."

Oil sprayed high into the air. This was called a "gusher"—but it was the first gusher American oil drillers had ever seen. Until then, American oil wells had come in with much less violence.

The north wind helped to spray areas downwind with a slick, slimy coating of oil. Later, when the wind changed and came from the south, oil covered houses and stores in Beaumont, too.

For nine days oil spewed into the air to a height equal to half a football field, and sometimes even higher. The gusher formed a giant lake of oil

around the drilling site. Finally, workers were able to control the spewing.

The large oil field that grew up around the hill south of Beaumont became known as "Spindletop." That first well became known as the "Lucas Gusher," and Pattillo Higgins, the "town fool" who had said that oil could be found where it was indeed discovered, was largely forgotten.

Spindletop gave up enough oil to leave a mark on world history. Oil eventually became the fuel for generating power for most ships, trains, and industries. And gasoline, which came from oil, would be available in enough quantity to fuel millions of automobiles and airplanes. The discovery at Spindletop provided oil in a great quantity not

known before 1901, and it showed Americans that a new source of energy had come into being.

Several of the largest oil companies in business today got their start at Spindletop. The Lucas Gusher and the many other oil wells drilled later in the Beaumont area made Texas famous as an oil-producing state. It also made many Texans wealthy, and it gave the state treasury a valuable source of income.

Oil, cattle, and cotton (as well as other farm crops) brought in much of the cash that Texans earned in the earlier part of the twentieth century.

But Texas had another important industry that is often overlooked today.

In East Texas an expansive pine-forested region covered all or part of forty-eight counties. This attracted men with a knowledge of the lumber industry. Settlers had begun cutting trees and selling the wood even before Texas won independence. Not until the 1880's, however, did the pine forests really begin to be harvested. That was because railroad expansion made it easier to ship the lumber to buyers outside of East Texas. After the turn of the century, men like John Henry Kirby and Jesse Jones made great fortunes in the lumber industry.

Lately the lumber industry has lost much of its importance. But in the early 1900's, lumber, ranching, and farming helped to keep many Texans living in rural areas of the state. After that, however, the oil industry brought many Texans to cities, so that today Texas is largely an urban state.

Oil caused this move to cities by fueling new manufacturing plants, which in turn attracted rural people who were looking for better jobs. Lumber and cattle industries never did pay workers very well, and usually provided only a bare existence.

Farming, too, has always been an unsure way of earning a living. Texas' often unpredictable weather can bring droughts that dry up crops, or it can bring heavy rains that flood crops, or cold spells that freeze crops. If the weather happens to

Tom Jones

be right, crops might be so large that the over-supply caused by this will bring prices down.

Many older Texans who grew up on farms can remember other problems besides the ones

brought on by disagreeable weather. In the earliest years of this century most rural homes, and even some homes in town, had no indoor plumbing. This meant that water for drinking, cooking, and washing had to be carried into the house somehow. There was no electricity and there were very few paved roads. And Texas' excessive heat made life very uncomfortable in the days before air conditioning.

Many Texans living now can remember two very unpleasant happenings of the earlier twentieth century.

First came a long period, in Texas and elsewhere, called the "Great Depression." Jobs and money became scarce for hundreds of thousands of Texans and for millions of Americans. This period began in 1929 and lasted for ten years or so.

One out of every five manufacturing plants in Texas went out of business. Farmers had to sell their cotton for six cents or less a pound instead of the eighteen cents a pound they had been getting. Oil became about as cheap as water.

In a December, 1933, edition of a Houston newspaper, the "help wanted" classified advertisements listed only three job openings for men and none at all for women. Despite the lack of jobs, some farmers moved to cities looking for work,

usually without success. If those people had stayed in the country they might have at least grown something to eat. Instead, they were often forced to line up with many other people to get free food from charity groups and to get other help from the United States government.

Hoboing and hitchhiking became a way of life for many men, some women, and even a few families. One out of every four Texans (and other Americans) wanting work couldn't find jobs. Many

TOM JONES

of them traveled—any way they could—trying to find work.

Some people turned to crime in order to get enough money to live on. Society has always had to deal with crime, of course. But in the early 1930's one of the worst crime waves in history hit Texas and the rest of the country. Two of the most famous criminals in Texas were named Bonnie Parker and Clyde Barrow. The pair traveled together. They were responsible for many robberies and murders before policemen shot them to death one morning in May, 1934.

In recent years "Bonnie and Clyde" have been rather glorified in books and films, but these stories are not based on truth. Honest accounts of the criminal career of Bonnie Parker and Clyde Barrow make it clear they were a cruel, cowardly pair who could kill helpless persons, then laugh about it.

There was another unpleasant happening of the earlier twentieth century that many older Texans can still remember. As if the Great Depression were not enough, a terrible drought hit Texas in the 1930's. Farmers and ranchers of the Panhandle and West Texas were especially hurt.

The earth dried, then winds blew away the topsoil. For several years during the 1930's large sections of Texas, Oklahoma, Kansas, Colorado, and New Mexico lay in the grip of what became known as the "Dust Bowl." Dark clouds of dust and sand would blow across the landscape, carry-

TOM JONES

ing away more topsoil and leaving behind—even inside homes—grimy coats of soil that had seeped through doors and windows.

Then the "black blizzards" (as these dust clouds were called) would blow on—usually eastward. In May, 1934, a very strong black blizzard roared eastward as far as New York City and

beyond. East of New York City, five hundred miles out in the Atlantic Ocean, crewmen aboard ships noticed dust settling on decks and railings of their vessels.

There were many other stories of black blizzards. Engineers operating train locomotives could not see railroad warning signals and would some-

times ram other trains or would tear into automobiles crossing the tracks. Sometimes the engineers couldn't even see the depots and would pass them by.

Elsewhere the worst storms paralyzed city traffic for hours at a time. They piled dust in some attics deep enough to cause collapse. And on at least one occasion, a storm blew so much powdery dust into a school gymnasium that a scheduled basketball game had to be called off.

Throughout this century, from the Lucas Gusher at Spindletop until today, the people of Texas have played major roles in events of national and even international importance.

When America entered the First World War in 1918, for example, Texas played a big part in the war effort. A lieutenant named Louis John Jordan was the first Texas officer killed in that war in which over five thousand Texans gave up

TOM JONES

their lives. Altogether, nearly 200,000 Texans served in the army or navy during World War I.

In the earliest years of this century women were not allowed to vote in Texas and in other states. In those days, most people believed that voting, earning a living, and other duties should be performed by men only. It was a Congressman from Texas named Morris Sheppard who introduced the law into Congress that would allow Americans to change the U.S. Constitution so that women could vote. Our Texas legislature approved this law on February 28, 1918.

Texas has provided more than its share of leaders to the nation. A poor Texas farm boy, Sam Rayburn, grew up to become one of the most powerful leaders in the country. Tennessee-born and Texas-bred, Sam helped to shape the nation and the world. When he was five his family left Tennessee and moved to Fannin County, Texas. Young Sam taught school for a while before he went into politics. His first public office was in the legislature in Austin. When he was elected to the national Congress, he stayed there for forty-eight years, twenty-one of those years as the Speaker of the House of Representatives. He held that important job longer than anyone else in history.

Barbara Jordan is another Texan who has helped shape the course of national events. She was a Congresswoman who touched the hearts of all Americans in a famous speech that was nation-

Barbara Jordan

ally televised. When the Congress was considering the impeachment of President Richard Nixon in 1974, Barbara Jordan made an eloquent speech that began with a well-known phrase, "We, the people . . . " and she spoke about the importance of the national Constitution.

Barbara Jordan had been born poor, the daughter of a black preacher, in Houston's Fifth Ward in 1936. But she rose above her humble beginnings and won fame and the respect of people everywhere. After serving in Congress, she returned to Texas to teach at the University of Texas at Austin.

Racial minorities enjoy rights and privileges in today's Texas that were lacking in earlier years. In the early 1900's, Texas and other states restricted blacks in a number of ways. One way was that blacks could not attend white schools—and of course, whites could not attend black schools either.

In public places, blacks were expected to use different facilities from those the whites used. For example, blacks had to sit in a different section of a public bus, eat at different restaurants or lunch counters, and drink from separate water fountains. This system of separation was called "segregation."

Blacks began to fight segregation in the 1960's, a struggle that came to be called the Civil

Rights Movement. One of the earliest leaders of this movement was a man named James Farmer, who was born in Marshall, Texas, in 1920.

Young James believed in the value of a good education, and he was able to attend Howard University in Washington, D.C. It was unusual for a black man to earn a college degree in those days. James graduated in 1942, and soon afterwards, with some friends, he formed an organization called the Congress of Racial Equality, or "CORE." Farmer's group helped to pave the way for the Civil Rights Movement of the 1960's. Although they wanted to "fight" injustice, James Farmer and other CORE members believed in nonviolent ways to win equal treatment for all men and women. They helped pave the way for a later civil rights leader, Martin Luther King Jr.

Another man who helped in a different way to improve the lot of blacks was Henry Allen Bullock. Henry was born in North Carolina in 1906. He chose a career in education and spent his life fighting to ensure that better education was available to blacks.

Henry Bullock taught social sciences at several mostly black colleges in the South. After forty years of teaching, he was asked to come to the University of Texas at Austin to teach a course called "The Negro in America." In 1970 he became a regular faculty member—the first black professor appointed to the faculty of arts and sciences at the university.

A United States president who was born in Texas helped blacks (and others) to get educations, too. He was President Dwight Eisenhower.

Eisenhower was born in Denison, Texas, October 14, 1890. He lived in Denison only a short time before his family moved to Kansas. But years later Texans proudly pointed him out as a native of the Lone Star State.

Eisenhower graduated from the United States Military Academy. Even before he was elected president he became world famous—as a general in the Army. He actually started on this road to fame early in the afternoon of December 7, 1941, while stationed at Fort Sam Houston, in San Antonio. Eisenhower was taking a nap in his home that day when his wife woke him with news that Japanese airplanes had attacked the United States Navy base at Pearl Harbor, Hawaii. Thus World War II began.

Audie Murphy

Dwight Eisenhower

Later Eisenhower, as a top commanding general, helped the United States and its allies win that war against Japan, Germany, and Italy. (Another Texan, Chester Nimitz of Fredericksburg and Kerrville, had a similar role as a Navy admiral, and Texans Audie Murphy and Macario Garcia won Congressional Medals of Honor for bravery in that War.)

Still later, after election as president in the

Chester Nimitz

1950's, Eisenhower—a Republican—helped the blacks by enforcing a Supreme Court decision that said black students and white students should attend the same schools instead of being segregated.

Another Texas-born president of the United States, Lyndon Baines Johnson, also helped to bring equal rights to all Americans, regardless of race. Johnson, who was a Democrat, used his presi-

Lyndon Johnson

dency in the 1960's to push much civil rights and education legislation through Congress. Johnson thus helped many blacks, Hispanics, and members of other minorities in today's society—not only in Texas but throughout the United States.

In the field of sports, medicine, music, and art, Texas has produced many people of great achievement. When the Associated Press—a national group of news reporters—chose the great-

est woman athlete of the half century 1900-1950, there was no doubt who would win. It was Mildred Ella Didrikson "Babe" Zaharias, who was born in Port Arthur in 1911 and grew up in Beaumont. At the 1932 Olympics in Los Angeles, there were five sports women could compete in, and one person could enter no more than three events. Babe won gold medals for the javelin throw and the eighty-meter hurdles, and she won a silver medal for the high jump.

She had been a star amateur basketball player as well as a baseball player on a men's team, but golf was the sport she eventually specialized in. She won over eighty tournaments. Babe Zaharias died in 1956 after fighting hard to beat cancer, but that disease finally defeated her.

People come from all over the world to the Texas Medical Center at Houston for some of the best and most advanced medical treatment. Heart surgeons like doctors Michael DeBakey and Denton Cooley are pioneers in their field as surely as were the early pioneers who braved the Indians and the wild weather and other hardships to settle Texas in the nineteenth century.

Aviation is another field in which Texans have made important contributions. Until the twentieth century, flying was only a dream for human beings. But at least two Texans were among

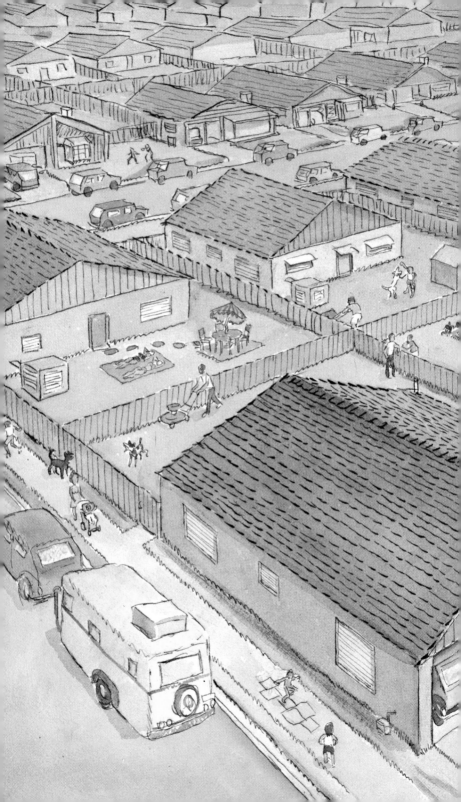

those who experimented with early flights in airplanes. Two brothers from the Midwest, Wilbur and Orville Wright, eventually were credited with making the first flight—in 1903.

Still, Texas stayed near the front in aviation progress. Soon after the invention of the airplane the United States Army established an aviation section at Fort Sam Houston, San Antonio, in 1910. The first man to fly across the Atlantic Ocean—Charles Lindbergh, in 1927—had graduated from the Army's flying school in San Antonio two years earlier.

Another aviation development in Texas concerns hurricane-hunting aircraft. Today airplanes fly routinely into those storms to get information for weather forecasting. But not until 1943 had an aircraft flown into a hurricane.

It happened off the Gulf Coast of Texas. The flight began on a dare. Some airmen stationed at Bryan Air Force Base, Texas, heard reports on July 27, 1943, that a hurricane was heading toward Galveston. Their talk led to wondering whether an aircraft then in use, the AT-6, could withstand such turbulent weather.

The base commander, Major Joe Duckworth, said he was certain the aircraft could survive such a storm. He recruited a reluctant second lieutenant, Ralph O'Hair, to accompany him as a navigator.

Forty minutes after taking off from Bryan, and after a fearfully rough flight, they reached the calm eye of the hurricane. They circled it twice. Then they flew back, safely, through more solid blackness, pounding rain, and roaring turbulence. They led the way for today's hurricane-hunters who gather storm information that can be had only by flying into the rough weather.

Texas has also had a major role in space flights, from the very first. A triumph in space by Soviet Russia hurried this along.

On October 4, 1957, Russia succeeded in sending the first man-made satellite into orbit. Then Russia launched a second satellite. Human beings did not go up in spacecraft then, because it wasn't known to be safe. But the second Russian satellite carried a dog, to see how animals would get along in space.

The successful launches by Russia hurried space work in America. The United States began spending much more money on its own program. Much of that money came to Texas. In the early 1960's the Manned Spacecraft Center opened about twenty-five miles from downtown Houston.

Today it has been renamed the Lyndon B. Johnson Space Center. Now, when a space flight is in progress, it is directed by men in the "Mission Control Center" at that space center.

In July, 1969, American astronauts became the first men to land on the moon. The first word to come from them was "Houston." The astronauts reported to the Mission Control Center, "Houston . . . the [spacecraft] *Eagle* has landed."

In the 1980's, progress in electronics has opened doors to new jobs and wealth. An industry called "High Tech"—for high technology—has come to several Texas cities during the current computer age. "High tech" industries make compact machines to serve people in various new ways with great speed and efficiency: calculators, digital watches, hand-sized televisions, and minicomputers are just a few examples.

A Texas man named Jack Kilby had a major role in bringing on this new industry. In 1958 he developed a tiny item called a silicon chip for the Texas Instruments corporation in Dallas. His silicon chip helped make possible all the new inventions that have changed people's lives.

Another Texan, H. Ross Perot of Dallas, founded a high-tech company called Electronic Data Systems which has become extremely successful. Perot has not been content only to found a very successful company. He has also worked hard to prevent drug abuse and recently has had a leading role in improving educational standards throughout Texas.

In recent years more people, industries, and money have been coming to Texas from other places. Texas' usually mild winters have attracted much of this. But so has air conditioning, which has become widely used since 1950. Air conditioning has made the hot Texas summers more bearable.

As Texas celebrates its 150th birthday since winning independence from Mexico in 1836, more growth seems certain. But no one should forget the part earlier Texans had in making the state what it is today. Their hard work during their frequently hard lives made living easier these days for most Texans.

The early Texans had little time for recreation. Staying alive was often a full-time job. They cleared land, extended the frontier, established homes and a government, and gave Texans of today many other benefits.

In the 1980's most Texans have money and time to read, listen to music, watch movies and television, and attend sports events featuring the Dallas Cowboys or Houston Astros or other athletic teams.

So, in this sesquicentennial year of 1986, Texans have reason to pause for a look backward to appreciate their roots, the colorful history that makes Texans different from any other people anywhere on earth.

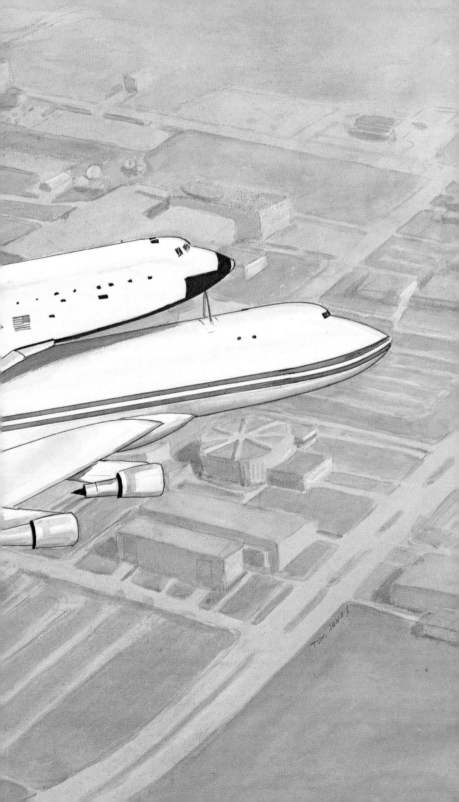

INDEX

215